SAINT-SAËNS

Sonata

Op. 167

for clarinet and piano

Edited by

Paul Harvey

CHESTER MUSIC

SONATA
FOR CLARINET AND PIANO

1

C.SAINT-SAËNS
Op.167
Edited by Paul Harvey

4

2

SAINT-SAËNS

Sonata

Op. 167

for clarinet and piano

Edited by

Paul Harvey

CHESTER MUSIC

SONATA
FOR CLARINET AND PIANO
1

Clarinet in B♭

C. SAINT-SAËNS
Op. 167
Edited by Paul Harvey

2

3

4

V.S.

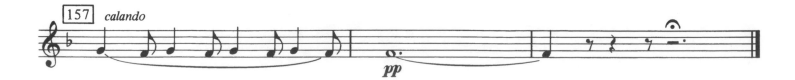

Camille Saint-Saëns (1835 - 1921) studied with Halévy and Gounod. He was organist at the Church of the Madeleine in Paris, and numbered Fauré among his pupils. He composed his Clarinet Sonata Op. 167 shortly before his death. It is dedicated to Auguste Périer (1883 - 1947), who was a professor at the Paris Conservatoire and Principal Clarinet at the Opéra Comique.

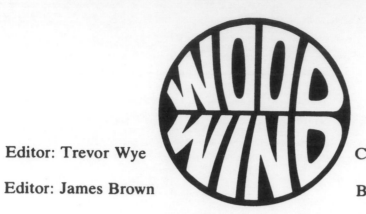

Flute   Editor: Trevor Wye   Clarinet   Editor: Thea King

Oboe   Editor: James Brown   Bassoon   Editor: William Waterhouse

A growing collection of volumes from Chester Music, containing a
wide range of pieces from different periods.

Order No: CH 55238

3

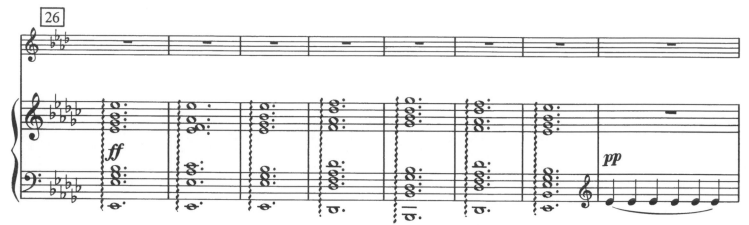

4

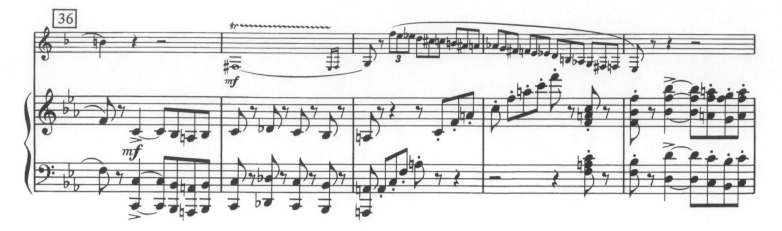